My Life as a Baby

This is my story!

My name _____

My birthdate _____

PETER PAUPER PRESS, INC.
White Plains, NY

PETER PAUPER PRESS
Fine Books and Gifts Since 1928

OUR STORY

In 1928, at the age of twenty-two, Peter Beilenson began printing books on a small press in the basement of his parents' home in Larchmont, New York. Peter—and later, his wife, Edna—sought to create fine books that sold at "prices even a pauper could afford."

Today, still family owned and operated, Peter Pauper Press continues to honor our founders' legacy—and our customers' expectations—of beauty, quality, and value.

Written by Virginia Reynolds
Illustrated by Terri Henson
Designed by Heather Zschock

Copyright © 2016
Peter Pauper Press, Inc.
202 Mamaroneck Avenue
White Plains, New York 10601
All rights reserved
ISBN 978-1-4413-2167-1
Printed in China
7 6 5 4 3 2 1

Visit us at www.peterpauper.com

Contents

My Baby Shower

(This is for my mother to fill in)

The baby shower was given by
....
(Name)

in
....
(Place)

at .... on ....
(Time)   *(Date)*

Guests
....

....

....

....

What it was like
....

....

Place photo from shower here.

All About My Family

I am _____ 's and
(My Mother)

_____ 's pride and joy.
(My Father)

I know my parents have these wishes and hopes for me
_____

_____

I'm the apple of everybody's eye (of course!), but especially

_____
(Maternal Grandmother)

_____
(Maternal Grandfather)

_____
(Paternal Grandmother)

_____
(Paternal Grandfather)

Place photo here.

My Vital Statistics

Important stuff to record for posterity (whatever that is)

I was born at   on
....
        (Time)   *(Date)*

in
....
                                                         (Place)

I weighed   and I was   long.
....
        (Weight)   *(Length)*

☐ I had hair. It was   ☐ I was as bald as an egg
....
                              (Color)

My eyes were an enchanting shade of
....
                                                            (Color)

I was especially cute because
....

....

....

☐ They said I looked perfect   ☐ They hoped I would grow into my looks
....

Place newborn photo here.

I was born...

☐ Head first ☐ Feet first ☐ Just like Julius Caesar

My condition was

People who were there when I made my debut included

Doctor

Nurse

Nurse

Moral support for my parents

Birth tests and results

Everybody's Talking

The first thing my mother said when she saw me was

The first thing my father said when he saw me was

They all said I looked like

The doctor said that I was

Other people said

The Early Days

My mother and I went home from the hospital on

....
(Date)

We lived at

....
(Address)

The people and pets waiting to welcome us were

....

....

What the first days at home were like

....

....

....

....

Photo of the Star

Place photo here.

Some of the very special people who visited me were

What my room was like

First Family Photo

Place photo here.

The World Around Me

When I Was Born...

The leader of my country was
....

The big news story of the day (besides my birth) was
....
....

Popular celebrities were
....
....

Movie that won the most awards was
....

Popular songs were
....

Hottest toy in the stores was
....

Price of one package of disposable diapers was
....

Place photo of nursery room
or home here.

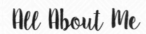

All About Me

My favorite blanket/comfort object was

....

....

I loved to play with

....

....

....

I looked so cute when I wore

....

....

I liked to go in the baby carriage to

....

....

....

People other than my parents who took care of me were

....

....

My first friends and playmates were

....

....

What was challenging

....

What was amazing

....

....

Glad Baby

Place photo here.

Mad Baby

Place photo here.

Special Event Commemorating My Birth

My christening, naming, bris, or other special event was
....

It happened on
....
(Date)

at
....
(Address)

People who shared my special event were
....

....

....

What it was like
....

....

....

That's me!

Place photo here.

Amazing Things About Me

I loved it when my mother
....
....

I loved it when my father
....
....

I always smiled at
....
....

I always giggled when
....
....

I sometimes cried when
....
....

The first solid food I ate was

....

on .... ☐ I loved it   ☐ I hated it   ☐ I spit it out

(Date)

I first ate from a spoon

....

I first drank from a cup

....

I began feeding myself for real

....

As I got older, I started to like

....

But I still hated

....

Some of my favorite foods were

....

....

....

Yum!

Place photo here.

Yech!

Place photo here.

How I Grew

FIRST MONTH   Weight   Length   Head circumference

Notes

SECOND MONTH   Weight   Length   Head circumference

Notes

THIRD MONTH   Weight   Length   Head circumference

Notes

FOURTH MONTH   Weight   Length   Head circumference

Notes

FIFTH MONTH   Weight   Length   Head circumference

Notes

SIXTH MONTH   Weight   Length   Head circumference

Notes

...And Grew

SEVENTH MONTH   Weight   Length   Head circumference

Notes

EIGHTH MONTH   Weight   Length   Head circumference

Notes

NINTH MONTH   Weight   Length   Head circumference

Notes

TENTH MONTH   Weight   Length   Head circumference

Notes

ELEVENTH MONTH Weight   Length   Head circumference

Notes

TWELFTH MONTH   Weight   Length   Head circumference

Notes

My List of World Records

The first time I...

Smiled

Laughed

Held my head up

Waved bye-bye

Rolled over

Slept through the night (hooray!)

Sat up

Crawled

Smile!

I got my first tooth on
....

▢ It was a breeze ▢ It was a storm
....

My other teeth eventually came in on

(Dates and Details)

....

....

....

....

....

Big Toothy Grin!

Place photo here.

My Likes and Dislikes

▢ I was a laid-back baby   ▢ I was a fussbudget

My favorite playtime activity was

The toy I liked best was

My favorite story was

The top song in my book was

Some other things I liked were

I'm having some serious fun here!

Place photo here.

Baby in the Tub

In the bath, I liked

But I wasn't crazy about

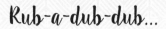

Rub-a-dub-dub...

Place photo here.

Sweet Dreams

At bedtime, I liked to relax by

But I didn't like to

This is how I slept

Sleeping baby—wasn't I precious?

Place photo here.

People and Places I Liked to Visit

Life of the Party!

Place photo here.

My First Holidays

The first holidays I celebrated were

....

....

....

....

And this is what they were like

....

....

....

....

Celebrate, Baby!

Place photo here.

Small Steps and Words of Wisdom

I pulled up to a standing position on

I cruised for the first time on

I took my first steps on

I liked to make these sounds

These were my first words (and when I said them)

Place photo here.

My First Birthday!

The birthday party was given by
....
(Name)

in
....
(Place)

at .... on ....
(Time)   *(Date)*

Guests
....

....

....

....

What it was like
....

....

Place photo of first birthday here.

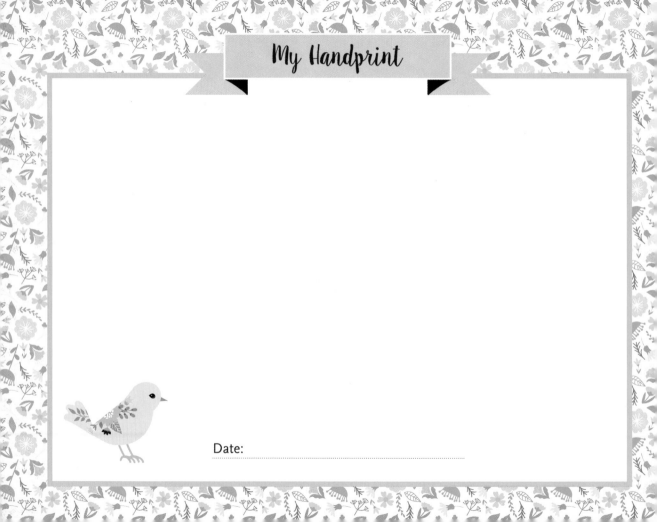

My Handprint

Date: ....